D0605191

Sample Pages Only

YOU CAN'T CAN'T READ THIS!

Why Books Get Banned

By Pamela Dell

Content Adviser: Richard E. Rupp, Ph.D., Interim Department Head, History and Political Science, Purdue University Calumet

Reading Adviser: Alexa L. Sandmann, Ed.D., Professor of Literacy, College and Graduate School of Education, Health, and Human Services, Kent State University

COMPASS POINT BOOKS
Camas Public Library

Compass Point Books
151 Good Counsel Drive
Box 669
Mankato, MN 56002-0669

Copyright © 2010 by Compass Point Books, a Capstone imprint
All rights reserved. No part of this book may be reproduced without written permission
from the publisher. The publisher takes no responsibility for the use of any of the
materials or methods described in this book, nor for the products thereof.
Printed in the United States of America in Stevens Point, Wisconsin.
072010
005879R

This book was manufactured with paper containing
at least 10 percent post-consumer waste.

Managing Editor: Catherine Neitge
Designer: Veronica Bianchini
Photo Researcher: Eric Gohl
Library Consultant: Kathleen Baxter
Production Specialist: Jane Klenk

Library of Congress Cataloging-in-Publication Data
Dell, Pamela.
  You can't read this! : why books get banned / by Pamela Dell.
      p. cm.—(Pop culture revolutions)
  Includes bibliographical references and index.
  ISBN 978-0-7565-4242-9 (library binding)
  1. Censorship—Juvenile literature. 2. Prohibited books—Juvenile
literature. I. Title. II. Series.
  Z657.D45 2010
  363.31—dc22   2009030749

Visit Compass Point Books on the Internet at www.compasspointbooks.com
or e-mail your request to custserv@compasspointbooks.com

Image Credits ©: American Library Association/Office for Intellectual Freedom, 56; AP
Images: 20, 23, 42–43, David Bookstaver, 58, Nam Y. Huh, 41, Sherin Zada, 10–11; The
Art Archive: Erin Pauwels Collection, 21, Topkapi Museum Istanbul/Gianni Dagli Orti, 15;
The Bridgeman Art Library: Archives Charmet/Private Collection/Lessing, Carl Friedrich,
46–47, Bibliotheque Nationale, Paris, France, 37, Crawford Municipal Art Gallery, Cork,
Ireland, 38–39, Museo de America, Madrid, Spain/Pre-Columbian, 13; Capstone Press,
29; Capstone Studio, 31, 57; Corbis: Bettmann, 49, EPA/Mohamed Messara, 16, Hulton-
Deutsch Collection, 24–25, 30; DVIC/NARA, 18; Getty Images: AFP/Saul Loeb, 27,
Hulton Archive, 22, National Geographic/Jean-Leon Huens, 36, Neil Jacobs, 4–5, 7, Tim
Boyle, 32, Time Life Pictures/Ed Clark, 45, Time Life Pictures/Heinrich Hoffmann, 54–55;
Library of Congress, 8, 14, 17, 28, 33, 44, 48, 50, 51, 52, 59; Newscom/KRT/Contra Costa
Times, 53, MCT/Detroit Free Press/Romain Blanquart, 40; Shutterstock: Andreas Guskos,
34, Carsten Reisinger, cover (padlock), Eky Chan, background, Fly, 19, Leigh Prather,
cover (book), Roman Sigaev, 1 (parchment), Tatiana Morozova, 1 (background), Vladimir
Melnikov, background, WOODOO, 3.

TABLE OF CONTENTS

From Pulp Fiction to Prizewinners

Adventures of Huckleberry Finn. The *Harry Potter* series. *Bridge to Terabithia*. *A Wrinkle in Time*. All books you'd find on your local library's shelves, right? Right.

But these famous and award-winning novels have something else in common. Although they are readily available in most schools and libraries, all have been challenged or banned again and again. So have a great many other important books. Why?

It seems to be a case of a self-appointed gatekeeper. Each of the books contains something, or some things, that someone has found upsetting. Those who want to ban books sometimes seem to be on a mission to save society, especially the youth. Their goal? To protect people from works that they consider inappropriate, dirty, dangerous, defiant, or otherwise offensive.

Members of a New Mexico church threw *Harry Potter* books into a bonfire in 2001 after their pastor called the books a "masterpiece of satanic deception."

But how are these books to be separated from other books? In other words, what's offensive? What's not? Maybe most important, who should determine what written works are OK and which are not? It's hard to imagine a day when everyone agrees on the answers to these questions.

Welcome to a never-ending struggle. On one side are the people who want to protect others from certain material. On the other side are those who don't want to be told—and don't want others to be told—what they can and can't read. And what about the writers? They simply want to say what they have to say. So what's the big deal?

Burned, Banned, and Challenged

Controversial books are often challenged, banned, or even burned. Everybody knows what burning and banning are. But what does it mean to challenge a book? According to the American Library Association, written challenges are "formal, written complaints filed with a library or school requesting that materials be removed because of content or appropriateness." Challenges sometimes lead to an official ban. Others succeed at first, but are later shot down. In most cases a challenge goes nowhere at all. But you can be sure that challenges will never stop!

A woman protested the burning of *Harry Potter* books in 2001 by church members in Alamogordo, New Mexico.

A poster condemning Nazi book burnings hung in U.S. bookstore windows during World War II.

Books cannot be killed by fire.

People die, but books never die. No man and no force can put thought in a concentration camp forever. No man and no force can take from the world the books that embody man's eternal fight against tyranny. In this war, we know, books are weapons. *Franklin D. Roosevelt*

BOOKS ARE WEAPONS IN THE WAR OF IDEAS

The big deal is that writers deeply value freedom of expression. They, more than most people, can put new ideas into words in powerful ways or express old ideas in new ways. As observers of society, writers make, break, and shake up pop culture. They give voice to ideas that can soothe the soul, make people furious, even change the world. Writers also serve as society's conscience. They speak the cold, hard truth as they see it, even though some people may find that truth uncomfortable or even painful.

Throughout history, writers and other artists have taken the lead in rebelling against authority and the status quo—the regular order of things. And many people have agreed with them. For some people, however, some works of "free expression" have been just a tad too free. They might even have been considered revolutionary. And guess what: This isn't just an attitude of the past. The pop culture revolution that books help to bring about is still happening. Curious? Just turn the page ...

Can You Guess?

Which author wrote these rebellious words?

"Be who you are and say what you feel, because those who mind don't matter and those who matter don't mind."

A. William Shakespeare

B. Dr. Seuss (Theodor Seuss Geisel)

C. Christopher Paul Curtis

D. J.K. Rowling

Find the answer on page 61.

CHAPTER 1
Censorship: It's Not Pretty

Book readers, beware! Those who ban books may be targeting what you want to read. Banning a book means not allowing others to read it or even have it.

The reasons for banning books are usually in one of four categories: religious, political, social, and sexual. Religious leaders ban works that they believe ridicule or contradict beliefs and practices that are sacred to their religion.

Political leaders ban works that they think might endanger or disrupt the government. Cultural watchdogs try to suppress books they fear will stir up unwanted social tensions or make people question the status quo. Parents and other people monitor books for sexual content and anything else they consider inappropriate or harmful.

Censorship on all these grounds is nothing new. It's gone on pretty much forever, on a global scale. Books become targets when they seem to pose a danger—to the existing political or social order, to morals, to established faith—or if they do not conform to accepted views and attitudes.

Books were burned at a girls school in Pakistan, one of nearly 200 schools attacked in 2008 by Taliban militants who do not want girls to be educated.

Books that accurately describe negative things about society are always at risk, too. Censored books fall into every category. Some are texts from the world's major religions, writings by the world's greatest philosophers, or scientific works.

Book banning is especially common in countries with authoritarian regimes, where a small group of leaders hold power. But even democracies sometimes impose this kind of censorship.

Authoritarian governments may grant some freedoms, but not any that will weaken their power or endanger their control. They are driven by the desire to stay in charge and enjoy the benefits of their power.

In democracies, on the other hand, the leaders are elected by the people and can be voted out of office. A constitution guarantees personal and political rights to everyone. So book banning shouldn't happen in countries with democratic governments, right? Yet it does.

Here are a few of the most disturbing examples of zealous censors who've declared war on the written word in times past. It's an unfortunate truth that the banning of expression has occurred—and continues to occur—in all religions and types of government.

THE SPANISH INQUISITION

The early Christian religion had several branches of thought. As Christianity grew and developed, the branch centered in Rome, Italy, began to dominate. Over many centuries this group's beliefs and writings became more and more established. Eventually the group became the Roman Catholic Church. The leaders of this powerful church began using extreme measures to prevent the spread of ideas that were not strictly in line with Catholic beliefs.

You probably wouldn't want to have been alive during the Spanish Inquisition, which the Catholic Church started in 1478. In fact, if you hadn't obeyed the religious authorities, you might not have lived through it. People were tortured, even gruesomely murdered, simply for having and expressing ideas that the church disapproved of.

In 1543, as part of the Inquisition, the church started banning books before they were even printed. It ruled that all the universities under its control could not print or sell any book without first getting the church's permission. The suppression lasted hundreds of years. It spread to every country under the church's control.

Maya Codex

One of the greatest losses in literary history was a collection of books called the *Maya Codex*. Spanish priests and conquistadors in Central America burned it during the 1500s. These books were sacred to the Maya people. They contained a detailed historical record of Maya culture. A few of the books escaped the flames and have found homes in museums in Europe and Mexico. But the record of an entire civilization was basically wiped out by this criminal destruction.

It's Everywhere

Book banning goes on in many countries around the world. Repressive religious and political authorities strictly control the kinds of information and ideas that are available to the public. The United States, however, has the First Amendment to the Constitution. This amendment protects the right to free speech and a free press. But how free is free? The First Amendment is in good working order. But even in this democratic society, suppression of ideas has a long, unpleasant history. It is still widespread.

Most students are familiar with the ongoing controversy over what they may or may not read. Quite a few could easily name at least one or two books that have been pulled from their school libraries' shelves. And it's not uncommon to hear of a teacher who had to fight to get some book included in the curriculum.

Censorship of books and other media is an act that generates resistance, a form of rebellion. Attempts to control people and enforce conformity are always met with a counterforce. It's human nature. And writers are at the forefront of that resistance, bringing their own individual ways of seeing the world. Sometimes their visions spark changes in some readers' minds. Sometimes they redirect pop culture. And once in a while, ideas put into the world through books cause unexpected, sweeping change— whether the books have been banned or not. In such cases, society often takes a giant step forward.

A 1953 political cartoon condemned attempts to censor books during the anti-Communist "Red Scare" of the 1950s.

ISLAMIC EXTREMISTS

The free exchange of ideas was an important feature of Islam during its early years. Although speaking out against the religion's leaders was not tolerated, controversial ideas were openly discussed and written about. This 500-year period, which lasted until 1258, was known as the Golden Age of Islam. But in the mid-1800s, printed materials became more widely available in Muslim countries. With the greater access, a new and more repressive trend began—a trend that continues today.

Many religious leaders objected to the availability of what they considered politically dangerous, anti-Islamic, or lewd writings. As radical religious leaders began to dominate some Islamic societies, the repression of free speech increased.

The nonprofit Middle East Media Research Institute has records documenting book bannings dating to 1925. The list of incidents is long. They include the censorship of dozens of books once considered essential parts of Islam's heritage. The banned works include important philosophical works of the past, books that favored the separation of religion and government, and even the great Islamic literary classic *One Thousand and One Nights*. Because these books are not easy to find in Muslim societies, many people have been robbed of much of their cultural history.

Ideas were freely discussed during the Golden Age of Islam.

Acts of violence against these works and their authors have often been extreme. In some Muslim countries, angry extremists have destroyed bookstores. Authors, publishers, and editors have been imprisoned, flogged, tortured, sentenced to death, or murdered. Some have even been beheaded. Most of the incidents have occurred in countries led by strict religious fundamentalists. The leaders want to keep everything they consider anti-Islamic from getting out into the world. But thousands of more moderate Muslims in the Middle East bravely continue to speak out and resist these repressive actions.

Algeria is host to an international book fair every fall.

THE SOVIET UNION AND EAST GERMANY

In 1926 the leaders of the Soviet Union sent a stern order to libraries throughout the country. It read: "The section on religion must obtain solely anti-religious books. Religiously dogmatic books such as the Gospel, the Koran, the Talmud, etc., must be left in the large libraries, but removed from smaller ones."

This was only a small part of the book-banning done over several decades in the Soviet Union. Among many other terrible acts, Soviet leader Joseph Stalin ordered entire collections of Jewish writings to be burned. This was an attempt to wipe out all written traces of the Jewish culture. Things were bad in communist East Germany, too. There, in 1953 alone, more than 5 million books were removed from libraries, bookstores, and schools. The books covered topics ranging from religion to democracy, and some were considered lewd.

A 1947 political cartoon suggested that Soviet actions were destroying hopes for peace.

Soldiers and civilians gave the Nazi salute as thousands of books burned in 1933.

NAZI GERMANY

In 1933 flaming pyres lit up more than one German city. In May student associations backed by the Nazi government staged huge book burnings. The destruction started in Berlin and spread across the country and into Austria. The goal was to eliminate all works considered "un-German." This included literature by Jewish authors, writings that criticized the Nazi dictatorship, and "degenerate art."

One of the most active youth groups involved in these destructive events was the Hitlerjugend, the fanatical, militarist youth organization of the Nazi Party. With the eager help of these young people, more than 25,000 books went up in flames in Berlin alone. They included many famous American titles, such as *The Call of the Wild* by Jack London, *The Sun Also Rises* by Ernest Hemingway, and *An American Tragedy* by Theodore Dreiser. Joseph Goebbels, the Nazis' minister of propaganda, praised the destruction. "From these ashes," he said, "will rise the phoenix of the new spirit."

COMMUNIST CHINA

During China's Cultural Revolution, in the late 1960s and early 1970s, censorship was common. China's entire educational system was shut down, and the country was in turmoil. Books were destroyed, teachers and intellectuals were attacked and killed, and the citizens were terrified. At the urging of Chairman Mao Zedong, radical young people calling themselves the Red Guards set out to destroy the "four olds": old thought, old culture, old customs, and old habits.

Mao's fanatical followers spread chaos and bloodshed throughout the country. Like Mao, they believed in the need for a violent revolution. The Red Guards charged into homes, museums, and temples, destroying books, works of art, musical instruments, and statues. Thousands of people were sent from cities to work in the countryside. Law and order disappeared. By the time Mao died in 1976, thousands had been killed, and an entire generation had gone without schooling.

Propaganda posters were common in China during the Cultural Revolution.

APARTHEID REGIME

For more than 40 years, the racist, repressive apartheid government of South Africa strangled free speech with widespread acts of censorship. Apartheid was South Africa's policy of racial segregation, under which blacks and other people of color were subjected to harsh discrimination. Extreme measures were used to silence the African National Congress and other political resistance groups. The white South African leaders banned many books, including some that had nothing to do with politics. One was the classic *Frankenstein*, by Mary Shelley. It was banned for being "indecent, objectionable, or obscene." At one point the government even banned *Black Beauty*. Why? Because the title of the famous children's novel about an abused horse had the word *black* combined with *beauty* in it. Most of the apartheid laws were repealed in 1990.

Ocean beaches were off-limits to non-whites in South Africa.

The Comstock Act

The Comstock Act of 1873 was named for the anti-obscenity campaigner Anthony Comstock (1844-1915). It outlawed the mailing of any material considered "obscene, lewd, and/or lascivious [lustful]." Included in the ban was information about birth control and abortion. Comstock was made a special agent of the U.S. Post Office Department and given wide-ranging power. He could simply walk into a post office and seize any material he did not approve of. Although they are not enforced, parts of the law are still on the books. At the end of his 40-year career, Comstock boasted of having destroyed nearly 160 tons (145 metric tons) of "offensive" written works. He also was proud of how many people he had sent to prison. The number, he claimed, was "… enough people to fill sixty-one coaches, with sixty of the coaches containing sixty people each and the last one almost full." In other words, almost 4,000 people.

A few masterpieces banned by the Comstock anti-obscenity law:

- Chaucer's *Canterbury Tales*
- Aristophanes' *Lysistrata*
- *The Arabian Nights*
- Books by Leo Tolstoy, Victor Hugo, William Faulkner, F. Scott Fitzgerald, Eugene O'Neill, and Honore de Balzac

A political cartoon in *Puck* magazine in 1891 condemned censorship after Leo Tolstoy's books were banned.

U.S. POSTAL SERVICE

Would it surprise you to know the U.S. Postal Service has been guilty of censorship? It's true. Its main targets have been books that were considered obscene or politically dangerous. In the two years before December 1941, when the United States entered World War II, the postal service repeatedly seized and destroyed shipments of books.

The books, mostly from Europe, were bound for American libraries. Between December 1940 and December 1941, postal authorities worked especially hard at cracking down. They destroyed more than 600 tons (546 metric tons) of written works coming to West Coast ports from foreign countries. The publications were burned on the spot.

Arthur Miller

In 1952, in the midst of a modern witch hunt seeking Communists, Arthur Miller wrote *The Crucible*. The play is about trials that occurred in Salem, Massachusetts, in 1692. During that time, people who did not live by society's rules were accused of being witches. They were put on trial and usually found guilty and punished. But the play had another layer of meaning. It seemed clear that it was meant to show how present-day congressional activities echoed what had happened in Salem 300 years earlier. Not surprisingly, the House Committee on Un-American Activities brought Miller in for questioning.

THE McCARTHY ERA

In the Cold War era, especially during the 1950s, free speech was again threatened in the United States. Government officials in Washington, D.C., led a massive effort to track down writers and others they suspected of favoring communism. This effort was started by U.S. Senator Joseph McCarthy of Wisconsin. At the same time, members of the House Committee on Un-American Activities were grilling anyone they considered even slightly suspicious. They encouraged people to report friends and family members who might have "un-American" thoughts or feelings. During this dark period in U.S. history, thousands of American citizens lost their jobs and good reputations. This was especially true in Hollywood. Countless screenwriters were banned from working, and their careers were destroyed, because of what came to be called the Red Scare.

Hollywood screenwriters headed for court in 1950 after they defied the House Committee on Un-American Activities.

CHAPTER 2
Bad Books!

Every time a book makes people think, act, or feel some strong emotion, watch out! The book just might cause a revolution. The possibility of that scares some people.

Hundreds of well-known works have been honored for their brilliant writing and their value to society. But many of them also have been attacked. Some highly respected books listed on the following pages show up repeatedly on censors' hit lists all over the world.

Boston police banned Communist literature in 1919, not long after the end of World War I.

THE BIBLE

The first printed book to be officially banned in England? The Bible. No joke. In 1525 and 1526, Catholic Church officials burned 6,000 copies of a translation of the New Testament. The problem was that this Bible was not an approved church version. But Bible banning began about 1,000 years earlier. In 533 the Roman emperor Justinian outlawed Bibles written in any languages other than Greek or Latin. Since then various versions of the Bible have been banned in other places. Usually it's a case of religious leaders' attempting to keep their flocks from straying. And it's not just the Bible. The Muslim Qur'an and the Jewish Talmud also have long histories of being banned.

Books on Trial

According to the American Library Association's Office for Intellectual Freedom, American libraries received 3,736 reports of challenges of books from 2001 through 2008. The office estimates that for every report of a challenge it received, another four or five challenges were never reported. Here are the reasons for some of the challenges (works may be challenged on more than one ground):

- 1,225 challenges for "sexually explicit" material
- 1,008 challenges for "offensive language"
- 720 challenges for material "unsuited to age group"
- 458 challenges for being "violent"
- 269 challenges for "homosexuality"
- 233 challenges because of "religious viewpoints"
- 103 challenges for being "anti-family"

Other reasons for challenges included "nudity," "racism," and "sex education."

HARRY POTTER SERIES

You might have guessed that books featuring wizards, demons, and magical happenings would cause an outcry by some people. And you'd be right—this is a common occurrence. The fear is that such books will send children on a wayward path, a path away from religious teachings. Harry Potter's champions argue that the series teaches kids strong positive values. They include trust, loyalty, friendship, and standing up for what's right and good.

Nevertheless, books in the *Harry Potter* series were seventh on the American Library Association's list of the 100 most often challenged books of 1990–2000. The series was just starting then. Between 2000 and 2007, *Harry Potter* had moved up the "Most Challenged" ranks to hold the top position. By 2008, however, it didn't even show up in the top 10. Not surprisingly, J.R.R. Tolkien's *The Lord of the Rings* series has also been challenged and banned. The arguments for and against these fantasies are the same as for the books in the *Harry Potter* series.

Two young women snapped up the final book in the *Harry Potter* series at a midnight sale in 2007 and read it on the steps of the Lincoln Memorial.

Pop Culture No-No's

Censors in the 20th century complained about more than books. Pop culture when your parents, grandparents, and great-grandparents were young was full of "dangers" that most people feel pretty much ho-hum about these days. Check out the list. At one time or another, they all prompted violent protests or bannings because of their perceived menace to society.

- motion pictures
- rock music
- radio jazz broadcasts
- comic books
- close dancing, slow dancing, and the "wild" dance style known as the jitterbug
- miniskirts
- long hair on guys

The jitterbug was wild, and popular, in 1943.

FAHRENHEIT 451

You've heard the expression "life imitating art"? It certainly applies here. Published by the renowned science fiction author Ray Bradbury in 1953, *Fahrenheit 451* is the story of a society in which thinking for oneself is considered a threat to the government. Therefore all reading material is banned.

Firefighters burn every book they can find. Fortunately there are a few rebels in this scary futuristic tale. Here's where life imitates art: Usually *Fahrenheit 451* is challenged because of its themes. In the book, and in real life, censors don't want people reading about freedom of expression, the free exchange of ideas, standing up to authority—or censorship!

Fahrenheit 451

The title *Fahrenheit 451* is significant. Paper burns at 451 degrees Fahrenheit.

A WRINKLE IN TIME

Published in 1962, *A Wrinkle in Time* by Madeleine L'Engle is an award-winning book that you may have read. This fantasy-sci-fi novel is frequently challenged. It is most often accused of having "offensive language" and "religiously objectionable" content. As in the *Harry Potter* books and other famous fantasy adventures, its characters include witches and demons.

A
WRINKLE
IN TIME

MADELEINE L'ENGLE

Edmond O'Brien starred in the movie version of *1984*, which was released in 1956.

PEOPLES
AREA
17

G BROTHER

WATCHING
YOU

being a Communist himself. In fact, he was anything but. The book paints a scary picture of life under such a government. It is a powerful argument against dictatorships.

BRIDGE TO TERABITHIA

This well-known book is also one you might have read. Or maybe you saw the 2008 movie version. In any case, a lot of people would like to keep kids from getting their hands on *Bridge to Terabithia*, Katherine Paterson's 1977 novel. This book about two children who create a magical kingdom won the Newbery Medal, the highest honor a book for children can receive. Yet *Terabithia* has been challenged or banned on several grounds. These include profanity, disrespect for adults, and creating an elaborate fantasy world that "might lead to confusion."

1984

Another book that would-be censors railed against, especially during the Communist-fearing 1950s, is *1984*. Published in 1949, George Orwell's *1984* is the story of a society ruled by Big Brother, a brutal dictatorship. Critics cried out that the book was pro-Communist, anti-Jewish, and "disrespectful to society." They accused Orwell of

Top Ten "Bad" Books

The 10 most-challenged books of the 21st century (2000–2007) are:

- *Harry Potter* series, by J.K. Rowling
- *Alice* series, by Phyllis Reynolds Naylor
- *The Chocolate War*, by Robert Cormier
- *Of Mice and Men*, by John Steinbeck
- *I Know Why the Caged Bird Sings*, by Maya Angelou
- *Scary Stories* series, by Alvin Schwartz
- *Fallen Angels*, by Walter Dean Myers
- *It's Perfectly Normal*, by Robie Harris
- *And Tango Makes Three*, by Justin Richardson and Peter Parnell
- *Captain Underpants* series, by Dav Pilkey

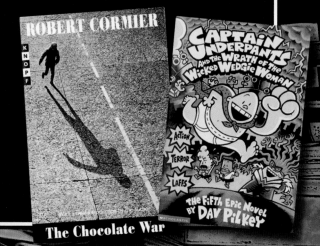

THE BIGGER PICTURE

Some banned or challenged books become targets because their critics zero in on details and ignore larger meanings. It might be a love scene with too many details. It is often a racial slur, or descriptions that show certain people or groups in a negative light. Such critics often overlook the powerful positive message that the books as a whole may convey.

Consider these two important examples: *Adventures of Huckleberry Finn* by Mark Twain (1884), sometimes called the greatest American novel, and the Pulitzer Prize-winning *To Kill a Mockingbird* (1960) by Harper Lee. Both of these classic novels have been challenged again and again. Even today there are frequent attempts to get them out of classrooms and libraries. To some extent, this is understandable. Both books deal with race relations and contain racist language no one wants to hear.

So why should they be read? As is true of many books, their authors have tried to give their works verisimilitude—to make their characters, places, and events seem real. In doing so, they have written scenes that, because they showed racism realistically, can be unpleasant to read. The critical point is that neither book promotes racism. They realistically reflect the times and places in which they were written and the settings of the stories they tell. In both cases, the overall stories argue powerfully for tolerance and acceptance between the races. Should such books be banned?

Huckleberry Finn

The books with Mark Twain's most famous characters, Tom Sawyer and Huckleberry Finn, have consistently been censored because they contain racist language, in particular the word "nigger." "[It] is an ugly word that ignites strong feelings and diminishes both speaker and hearer," wrote Craig Lancto, a former English teacher and author of *Banned Books: How Schools Restrict the Reading of Young People*. "Of course, neither Huck nor Tom meant it in a derogatory way. It was what they heard adults of their day say. Their behavior did not reflect racism, but those who would ban the book [*Adventures of Huckleberry Finn*] because of it rob students of the opportunity to discover that Twain was not a racist. Instead, they [increase] racial tensions by finding racism where it does not exist. … The real tragedy is that [young readers] will remember Mark Twain as a racist instead of experiencing [the slave] Jim's goodness and Huck's attitude toward Jim, when they escaped Hannibal on a raft."

CHAPTER 3

Authors Who Outrage

Long ago in ancient Athens, a rebellious
guy got the public really stirred up.
He was the great philosopher Socrates,
who lived in the 400s B.C.
If Socrates ever
wrote down any of
his ideas, those
writings
have not
survived.

All we know about his thoughts and his life come to us from his students, including the equally great Plato. There's a good chance, however, that people then banned or destroyed anything Socrates may have written.

They would have destroyed his work because Socrates strode the streets of ancient Athens encouraging young people to think for themselves. He showed them how important it is to question everyone and everything, including authority—just as he continually did.

Not surprisingly, the adults in Athens did not appreciate what he was doing. It alarmed the government, too. Socrates was put in prison and sentenced to die by drinking the poison hemlock.

Thinkers of every kind have been dogged by disapproval. Here is a look at two rebels from centuries past and some of America's best-known targets from recent decades.

GALILEO GALILEI

Now here's a farsighted thinker from yesteryear. Galileo Galilei got into trouble with the Catholic Church in 1633. He was tried in the Italian courts and convicted. Galileo's supremely rebellious act? He published *Dialogue Concerning the Two Chief World Systems*. His book argued that Earth revolved around the sun rather than the sun around Earth, as most people thought. According to Catholic beliefs of the time, Earth was unquestionably the center of the universe. New theories such as Galileo's challenged religious doctrine. Church authorities did not want anyone but themselves announcing new ideas that could change religious belief. Any defiance of this policy was punished.

Galileo was put under house arrest. He gradually grew blind and died nine years after his conviction. His infamous text was included in the *Index of Prohibited Books* until the 1800s. Not until 1992 did church authorities admit their error— that Galileo had been right about Earth's orbit.

Church leaders did not believe Galileo's theories.

Index Librorum Prohibitorum

The *Index Librorum Prohibitorum* (*Index of Prohibited Books*) was the brainchild of Pope Paul IV. He created it in 1559, and it was in force until 1966. The authors and titles on this banned-books list were considered dangerous. Their ideas did not go along with Catholic beliefs. So all Catholics were forbidden to read anything on the list.

Throughout the centuries, popes continued to issue new lists. Altogether there were 42 *Indexes*, with the last published in 1948. It included 4,000 titles off-limits to members of the church. Today, even without the official list, Catholics are still commanded to "avoid writings which can be dangerous to faith and morals."

WILLIAM SHAKESPEARE

Shakespeare has often been censored. His plays *Hamlet, King Lear, Macbeth, Twelfth Night,* and *The Merchant of Venice* seem to take the most heat. The charges are usually "adult language," sexual content, or violence (*Hamlet, Macbeth, King Lear*). Another common complaint is anti-Semitism (*The Merchant of Venice*), in this case showing Jewish characters in unflattering or hateful ways.

Need proof that if you want to censor something, you can find a reason? In a 1996 case in Merrimack, New Hampshire, *Twelfth Night* was removed from the curriculum by the school board. The board decided that the play violated its ban on "alternative lifestyle instruction"—because a female character in the play disguises herself as a boy! By 1999 Merrimack had voted those school board members out of office, and *Twelfth Night* was back in the classrooms.

Shakespeare Bowdlerized!

In 1807 a British doctor, Thomas Bowdler, published a book called *The Family Shakespeare*. It included 24 of Shakespeare's plays in cleaned-up form: Bowdler had employed his sister to remove or rewrite passages. Their aim was to get rid of everything Bowdler didn't think families should be reading. This included "dirty language." Many love scenes had to go, too.

Several even larger editions appeared later. Bowdler defended the censored works. His goal, he said, was simply to remove "everything that could give offense to the religious and virtuous mind." Today the word bowdlerize means prudish censorship.

Shakespeare's *King Lear* has come under fire for its references to sex and violence.

JUDY BLUME

Does this name surprise you? Judy Blume is one of America's best loved—and most banned—modern authors of books for young people. The American Library Association reported in 2004 that she was the second most censored author of the previous 15 years. (Alvin Schwartz, author of the *Scary Stories* series, was first.) Five of Blume's titles hit the "hot 100" of most frequently challenged books during the 1990s. If you've read her work, you might have an idea of why. Blume writes frankly and realistically about important topics that kids relate to. But some adults feel she's too frank. They also may not like the fact that Blume speaks out with a passion for the right of young readers to read freely. She does not believe in censorship, of her books or anyone else's.

Judy Blume signed a book from her series *The Pain and the Great One* for a young fan.

and **tango**
makes
three

by Justin Richardson
and Peter Parnell
Cole

Challenged Books

The ALA's Top 10 most frequently challenged books of 2008

1 *And Tango Makes Three,*
   by Justin Richardson
   and Peter Parnell

2 *His Dark Materials Trilogy,*
   by Philip Pullman

3 *TTYL; TTFN, and L8R, G8R*
   series, by Lauren Myracle

4 *Scary Stories* series,
   by Alvin Schwartz

5 *Bless Me, Ultima,*
   by Rudolfo Anaya

6 *The Perks of Being*
   a Wallflower,
   by Stephen Chbosky

7 *Gossip Girl* series,
   by Cecily Von Ziegesar

8 *Uncle Bobby's Wedding,*
   by Sarah S. Brannen

9 *The Kite Runner,*
   by Khaled Hosseini

10 *Flashcards of My Life,*
   by Charise Mericle Harper

ALLEN GINSBERG

Allen Ginsberg was a leading poet in a group of 1950s writers who were known as the Beat Generation. His most famous work, the poem "Howl for Carl Solomon," was published in 1956. With that poem, this bearded beatnik became the 1950s' major symbol of youthful rebellion against what was called "the establishment"—the traditional ruling class. "Howl," as the poem is usually known, became a pop culture triumph. It also caused an immediate, outraged howl of "obscenity!"

The poem is a long, blistering attack. It targets the materialistic, conformist tendencies Ginsberg saw in the post-World War II society around him. The straightlaced folks of the day did not appreciate the poet's defiance—or the poem's graphic language and imagery. Soon after its publication, "Howl" was banned in the United States on charges of obscenity. Later, after the ban was lifted, its value to society was widely recognized. New York writer Sam Kashner called it "a poem to heal and change lives. It's a profoundly great work."

"Howl" Still Howling

In 2007 a U.S. radio station attempted to air a reading of "Howl." Fifty years earlier, in October 1957, a court had ruled the poem was protected against charges of obscenity by the First Amendment. The Federal Communications Commission stepped in and stopped the 2007 broadcast. The censorship troubled a lot of people. A lawyer for the American Civil Liberties Union said, "It's no longer accurate to say free speech has rolled back to the fifties. It's worse now. A radio station cannot possibly celebrate the First Amendment by being forced to gag its announcers."

Allen Ginsberg read poetry to a crowd in a New York City park in 1966. Ginsberg and other poets were testing a court ruling on censorship.

JOHN STEINBECK

John Steinbeck was a renowned Nobel Prize-winning author. He often wrote about the hard lives of migrant workers, the poor, and others downtrodden by society. Two of his novels on these topics have been repeatedly challenged over the years. One is *Of Mice and Men* (1937), a novel about the friendship between two men, one mentally disabled. It is usually challenged on the ground of offensive language.

The Grapes of Wrath (1939) has been through perhaps even more challenges. It was most vigorously challenged in Kern County, California. This is because it is a story about a poor family that, during the Depression, leaves Oklahoma and tries to make a living in Kern County. The novel clearly shows that the migrant farmworkers are unjustly treated by powerful landowners. Those who sought to ban it claimed it "offended our citizens." While its purpose was not to offend, it probably did. The citizens were not shown in a positive way. Another word frequently found in challenges against Steinbeck is "vulgar."

Dorothea Lange's 1936 photograph *Migrant Mother* captured the hopelessness of the Depression.

TONI MORRISON

Novelist Toni Morrison has won both the Pulitzer and Nobel prizes for literature. This makes her one of America's most acclaimed and important authors. But challenges to her books continue to occur. Two of the titles frequently under fire are her first novel, *The Bluest Eye* (1970), and *Beloved* (1987). *The Bluest Eye* is often challenged for its strong sexual content and language that some find offensive. Many readers are disturbed by *Beloved*'s depiction of some of the most terrible aspects of slavery. Other charges have included its being "trashy," "obscene," and "anti-white."

RICHARD WRIGHT

Richard Wright was born into a poor sharecropper's family in the segregated South of 1908. As an angry, intelligent young man, he believed that "books are weapons." His writings often focused on themes of politics, sex, and race. *Native Son*, a novel published in 1940, and his 1945 autobiography, *Black Boy*, were two of the first books that described the worst effects of racism. *Black Boy* was banned from American schools from 1975 through 1978. Censors called it obscene and feared its potential to "instigate hatred between the races."

Wright's brutally real depictions of racial conflict and injustice still shock readers. Nevertheless, his work is widely recognized for its high literary quality. *Native Son* and *Black Boy* continue to face challenges. These days the grounds are usually violence, profanity, and inappropriate sexual content.

Life magazine featured a photo documentary about Richard Wright when *Black Boy* was published in 1945.

CHAPTER 4

Changing the World

Every now and then, a banned book contains ideas that sweep through society like ripples on a windblown lake. When that kind of momentum occurs, get ready!

The author's message may bring about a revolution in thought—a shift in perceptions, beliefs, or values among large numbers of people. Books like that sometimes even change the world.

Here are three important authors who had that kind of effect. Their works rocked the established order like literary tidal waves, bringing major social changes.

MARTIN LUTHER

This rebel had a cause that succeeded perhaps beyond his wildest dreams. Martin Luther was born in 1483 in Germany. The area where he lived was under the control of the Holy Roman Empire. So, like everyone else in the region, he grew up a Catholic. He even became a priest.

As a studious and observant young man, Luther was shocked by the behavior of some church officials, who he and many others thought were immoral and corrupt. He began speaking out against the pope, the leader of the Catholic Church. Though it was dangerous to do so, he started publishing works critical of Catholic practices and beliefs. His list of criticisms of the church—called *Ninety-Five Theses*—is one of the earliest and most famous of these.

Martin Luther burned a message from Rome in defiance of the pope.

Luther's passionate protests fired up many of his peers. His ideas caught on and quickly spread, even though the church did its best to prevent that from happening. Authorities banned and burned Luther's books and pamphlets, particularly his translations of the New Testament of the Bible. Still, his ideas about God and church were accepted far and wide. This gave rise to the Protestant Reformation and great intellectual progress in the following centuries. Luther's mind was the birthplace of Protestant theology. At the same time, however, many of his writings were anti-Semitic, and they have been condemned by modern Lutherans.

HARRIET BEECHER STOWE

When Harriet Beecher Stowe published her anti-slavery novel *Uncle Tom's Cabin* in 1852, there was an immediate uproar. Her vivid story of slave life in the South shocked and horrified Northerners. Few of them had given the issue of slavery much attention before then. The book challenged people's consciences. Overnight it turned many into abolitionists—people who supported the banning of slavery.

In the South things were different. *Uncle Tom's Cabin* was widely outlawed in slaveholding states. Southerners objected to the depiction of their way of life.

An 1879 woodcut with scenes from *Uncle Tom's Cabin*

Pop Culture Mainstay

Uncle Tom's Cabin has an impressive record. Within a week of its publication, its sales had already reached 10,000 copies. Within a year the total was 300,000 copies. Only five years after it first appeared, the book was available in 20 languages. Adaptations of the story appeared constantly in other media as well. They still do today. *Uncle Tom's Cabin* was the second-best-selling book of the 1800s. The only book that outsold it during that century was the Bible.

135,000 SETS, 270,000 VOLUMES SOLD.

UNCLE TOM'S CABIN

FOR SALE HERE.

AN EDITION FOR THE MILLION, COMPLETE IN 1 Vol. PRICE 37 1-2 CENTS.
"   "   IN GERMAN, IN 1 Vol, PRICE 50 CENTS.
"   "   IN 2 Vols, CLOTH, 6 PLATES, PRICE $1.50.
SUPERB ILLUSTRATED EDITION, IN 1 Vol, WITH 153 ENGRAVINGS,
PRICES FROM $2.50 TO $5.00.

The Greatest Book of the Age.

Some even claimed that the book greatly exaggerated the way things were. It didn't.

"So you," President Abraham Lincoln is said to have told Stowe, "are the little lady who wrote the book that started this great war." This is not far-fetched. The novel widened a chasm between North and South that led to the Civil War (1861–1865).

Now, as then, the novel is both celebrated and condemned. Among other complaints, challengers today note the negative racial stereotypes it reinforced. They especially dislike the Uncle Tom character because he is portrayed as a subservient, powerless black man. Indeed, "Uncle Tom" is still a derogatory term. It means a black person who is too eager to please white people. Another frequent challenge to the book is that it uses racist language.

Despite these concerns, *Uncle Tom's Cabin* was a breakthrough in its day. Its publication was perfectly timed. The novel dramatically and profoundly shifted the way many Americans thought about slavery. It brought important cultural changes to the United States.

UPTON SINCLAIR

Muckraker was a term used often by President Theodore Roosevelt. Although at first its definition wasn't flattering, it came to mean a writer who exposed corruption, big-business abuses, and other unethical behavior. Upton Sinclair, a writer in Roosevelt's time, certainly was a muckraker—of the most effective kind.

Sinclair's novel *The Jungle* was published in 1906. It tells the story of poor immigrants who end up working in Chicago's meatpacking industry.

Although it is a work of fiction, the horrific details were straight from real life. Shortly after it came out, President Roosevelt sent a government team to Chicago. Their task was to confirm the terrible conditions depicted in the book.

Sinclair exposed for the first time the filthy, rat-infested environment in which America's meats were processed. He described in detail the extreme abuses suffered by employees in that industry. He showed how grim and dangerous their work was.

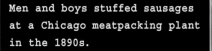

Men and boys stuffed sausages at a Chicago meatpacking plant in the 1890s.

As with Stowe's book, *The Jungle* caused immediate outrage. Corporate bosses weren't happy about readers' seeing inside their industry. Now the victimization of workers by unregulated big business was known to all. Other people couldn't stand the way Sinclair so obviously put forth his socialist political views. He strongly favored unionizing labor. He also championed social welfare for the poor and downtrodden, especially those who were taken advantage of by wealthy corporate bosses. Through his writing, Sinclair sided with the have-nots, and he showed the haves—those in control of society—in the most unflattering light. In Boston and other cities, the Catholic Church banned *The Jungle*, saying it contained inappropriate sexual content.

Sinclair's novel was later censored in many other parts of the world, often for political reasons. It was banned from Yugoslavian libraries in 1929. It was burned by the Nazis in the 1930s and banned in East Germany in the 1950s. South Korea banned the book in the 1980s.

THE JUNGLE
BY
UPTON SINCLAIR

DOUBLEDAY, PAGE & C°
NEW YORK

The Jungle

Like *Uncle Tom's Cabin*, *The Jungle* was first serialized over many months in a magazine. One segment mentions Harriet Beecher Stowe. Not surprisingly, Upton Sinclair said he modeled his novel after her classic work.

The government sent inspectors to Chicago in 1906, following publication of *The Jungle*.

Nevertheless, the book's publication brought about long-lasting social good. Roosevelt and Congress quickly put into law the Pure Food and Drug Act and the Meat Inspection Act. As a result, the U.S. Food and Drug Administration was formed. Today the FDA makes sure foods Americans buy are manufactured under sanitary conditions and are safe to eat. Sinclair did not consider his work a total success, however. Getting banned made him richer, but that wasn't his real goal. He said, "I aimed for the public's heart but by accident I hit it in the stomach." He had hoped to change the plight of the real-life struggling people in the meatpacking industry. The workers never got much attention, though. Everybody was too upset and disgusted about how meat was produced.

The Jungle Redux

Redux means "brought back." That seems to be what's happening in some parts of the meatpacking industry today. Modern muckraker Eric Schlosser published *Fast Food Nation* in 2001. He says you might not want to know "what really lurks between those sesame seed buns" at your local fast food joint. Schlosser's book is nonfiction, and so far no one's banned it. Still, like *The Jungle*, it probably didn't make industry insiders happy.

Fast Food NATION

Eric Schlosser

The Dark Side of the All-American Meal

CHAPTER 5

The Fight for Reading Freedom

"Free people read freely." The slogan of the Freedom to Read Foundation says it all. Intellectual freedom—the freedom to read, write, think about, and discuss ideas—is a right held dear.

After all, if we don't work to uphold this basic human right, what might happen? How long would it take before we were all living in a *Fahrenheit 451* society? Should we all be thinking exactly alike? Is it dangerous to consider opinions or ideas different from ones we were brought up with, or ones held by a majority? Should people whose opinions we dislike be silenced?

Book censorship is a complicated, controversial matter. As time goes on and society changes, the uproar around some challenged books dies down. Some banned books eventually become beloved books. Others end up both banned and beloved by opposing groups at the same time. A number of titles seem to remain in the sights of the censors no matter how much time passes. The question of where to draw the line remains.

First Amendment

So what is this First Amendment to the U.S. Constitution we keep talking about? Here it is:

Congress shall make no law respecting an establishment of religion, or prohibiting the free exercise thereof; or abridging the freedom of speech, or of the press; or the right of the people peaceably to assemble, and to petition the government for a redress of grievances.

Germans and others endured more than 10 years of brutal Nazi rule. Millions lost their freedoms and their lives.

Banned Books Week: Celebrating the Freedom to Read

For one week every September, an important event takes place across the United States. Bookstores and libraries celebrate the freedom to read. Banned Books Week is sponsored by the American Booksellers Association, the American Library Association, and other organizations that support free speech. By staging events and gaining publicity, these book lovers raise public awareness. They bring attention to the dangers of restricting people's choices in what they read. Next time Banned Books Week happens, get involved. Read a banned book or two!

The Lorax, by Dr. Seuss was challenged for "criminalizing the foresting industry."

BANNED BOOKS WEEK
Celebrate Your Freedom to Read
www.ala.org/bbooks

Balancing Act

Uninformed people are easier to control. That's a fact. Some governments and religious authorities-and parents-obviously consider this a good thing. And too often, fear and misinformation drive the impulse to ban books.

On the positive side, of course, adults have a powerful natural instinct to protect the young. You have probably read books that you wouldn't feel comfortable giving to younger kids. We all know that not every book is suitable for every person. Most people agree that parents should direct their children to or away from reading material based on their knowledge of each child. But should they, not to mention government officials, also decide what's appropriate for other people's children?

THE CATCHER IN THE RYE J. D. SALINGER

THE GOLDEN COMPASS PHILIP PULLMAN

A SEPARATE PEACE JOHN KNOWLES

Nineteen Eighty-four George Orwell

Lord of the Flies William Golding

SLAUGHTERHOUSE-FIVE KURT VONNEGUT, JR.

JOHN STEINBECK THE GRAPES OF WRATH

HARRY POTTER AND THE PRISONER OF AZKABAN

TONI MORRISON BELOVED

PILKEY CAPTAIN UNDERPANTS and the Wrath of the Wicked Wedgie Woman

PATERSON BRIDGE TO TERABITHIA

TO KILL A Mockingbird HARPER LEE

CORMIER The Chocolate War

ULYSSES JAMES JOYCE Modern Library

JOHN STEINBECK East of Eden

MAURICE SENDAK IN THE NIGHT KITCHEN

COLLI

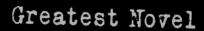

Greatest Novel

In 2006 *The New York Times* asked leading U.S. writers, critics, and editors to take a vote. What, asked *The Times*, is the greatest work of American fiction published in the last 25 years? When all the votes were in, Toni Morrison's *Beloved* had been ranked number one by her peers.

Social responsibility is another topic closely tied to First Amendment rights. In the case of books, that means being aware of how written works might affect others. There is always a long list of books challenged because of their unflattering—or even hateful—portrayal of some ethnic, religious, or political group. Related to this is the question of language, such as the use of racial or ethnic slurs. Most of these challenges are related to books that turn up in school classrooms or on school library shelves.

No reasonable person wants to live in a society where disrespect, bigotry, intolerance, or plain, ugly hatred rule, or are even accepted. So here's the big question: How do we balance the importance of students' receiving a bigotry-free education, in a nonhostile environment, with the need to allow everyone their First Amendment rights? What offends one may not offend another. Who should decide what we can read?

It is one thing to dislike or disagree with the viewpoint expressed in an author's work. It is quite another matter to make the material unavailable to everyone else.

Where Do
You Stand?

When young people, under the thoughtful guidance of adults, are given the chance to choose for themselves what to read, something good happens. They become better and better at making their own wise decisions and choices. It can also be argued that students with access to a wide selection of competing ideas learn to analyze information and think critically. This applies not only to what they have read but also to what goes on in the world around them.

Through this process of education based on intellectual freedom, young people begin to know who they are and what they stand for. This may be the best payoff of all. They become truly themselves, not simply a copy of someone else.

The United States is an amazingly diverse nation. It's composed of many cultures, religions, languages, philosophies, ethnicities, beliefs, colors, and creeds.

"One Book That Can't Be Burned," a 1953 political cartoon by Edwin Marcus

All the voices that rise from this remarkable mix and find their way into books must be available to whoever might be interested in them. This is what the First Amendment assures us. Writers can shake things up by crafting stories or documenting situations we may not want to read about and giving us thoughts we may not want to have. It is up to everyone to fight against the silencing of any of those voices, like them or not. If we don't, our own voices might someday be silenced, too.

Where do you stand?

Timeline

533 •••••••••••••• The Roman emperor Justinian outlaws Bibles in any language except Greek and Latin

1235 •••••••••••• Pope Gregory IX orders the destruction of all works containing ideas that differ from Catholic beliefs; some authors are executed

1517 •••••••••••• Martin Luther's *95 Theses* is banned for being critical of Catholicism, leading to the establishment of Protestantism

1559 •••••••••••• Introduction of the *Index Librorum Prohibitorum* by the Roman Catholic Church

1641 •••••••••••• The Tokugawa dynasty in Japan establishes widespread censorship policies that last 200 years

1796 •••••••••••• British citizens form the Society for the Suppression of Vice, which engages in massive book banning

1873 ••••••••••••The Comstock Act, an attempt to keep obscenity out of the U.S. mail, becomes law

1933 •••••••••••• Massive book burnings take place across Germany and Austria

1940-1941 •••• U.S. postal authorities seize more than 600 tons (546 metric tons) of books entering American ports

1950s •••••••••••• Senator Joseph McCarthy leads a campaign to ban more than 300 books he says have "communist influence"

1982 •••••••••••• The American Library Association sponsors the first Banned Books Week

1989 •••••••••••• British author Salman Rushdie's novel *The Satanic Verses* is banned and burned in many countries for being "anti-Islamic"

2007 •••••••••••• The *Harry Potter* series tops the list of most challenged books in the U.S.

2009 •••••••••••• Author Herta Mueller, who was censored in her native Romania, wins the Nobel Prize in literature

Glossary

Cold War	period of tension between the United States and the Soviet Union that did not result in combat
controversial	causing dispute or disagreement
degenerate art	artworks that the Nazis believed showed symptoms of moral and social decline
derogatory	tending to lessen the merit or reputation of something or someone
doctrine	set of religious beliefs
fundamentalist	person who believes unquestioningly in a set of basic and unchangeable religious ideas
lewd	indecent or obscene
muckraker	person who looks for injustice, corruption, or scandal, often for the purpose of publishing the information
pyre	pile or heap of material to be burned
subservient	overly submissive; willing to do what others demand
suppress	to prevent from being revealed or published
zealous	extremely eager or enthusiastic

Answer to quiz on page 9

B. Dr. Seuss (Theodor Seuss Geisel)

Additional Resources

Crutcher, Chris. *The Sledding Hill*. New York: Greenwillow Books, 2005.

Cushman, Karen. *The Loud Silence of Francine Green*. New York: Clarion Books, 2006.

Hardinge, Frances. *Fly by Night*. New York: HarperCollins Publishers, 2006.

Haynes, Charles C., et al. *First Freedoms: A Documentary History of First Amendment Rights in America*. New York: Oxford University Press, 2006.

Karolides, Nicholas J. *Literature Suppressed on Political Grounds*. New York: Facts on File, 2006.

Lankford, Ronnie D., ed. *Book Banning*. Detroit: Greenhaven Press, 2008.

MacDonald, Joan Vos. *J.K. Rowling: Banned, Challenged, and Censored*. Berkeley Heights, N.J.: Enslow Publishers, 2008.

Paxton, Mark. *Censorship*. Westport, Conn.: Greenwood Press, 2008.

Ross, Val. *You Can't Read This: Forbidden Books, Lost Writing, Mistranslations, and Codes*. New York: Tundra Books, 2006.

Sova, Dawn B. *Literature Suppressed on Social Grounds*. New York: Facts on File, 2006.

Tracy, Kathleen. *Judy Blume: A Biography*. Westport, Conn.: Greenwood Press, 2008.

FactHound

FactHound offers a safe, fun way to find Internet sites related to this book. All of the sites on FactHound have been researched by our staff.

Here's all you do:
Visit *www.facthound.com*
FactHound will fetch the best sites for you!

Look for the other books in this series:

- GAMERS UNITE!
  The Video Game Revolution

- PLAY IT LOUD!
  The Rebellious History of Music

- GRAPHIC CONTENT!
  The Culture of Comic Books

Select Bibliography

"75th Anniversary of the Nazi Book Burnings: Interview with Matt Fishburn." AbeBooks. 25 June 2009. www.abebooks.co.uk/docs/Community/Featured/book-burning-fishburn.shtml

"100 Most Frequently Challenged Books: 1990–1999." American Library Association. 16 Oct. 2009. www.ala.org/ala/issuesadvocacy/banned/frequentlychallenged/challengedbydecade/1990_1999/index.cfm

"American Poet Allen Ginsberg." National Coalition Against Censorship. 29 June 2009. www.thefileroom.org/documents/dyn/DisplayCase.cfm/id/1149

Baez, Fernando. *A Universal History of the Destruction of Books: From Ancient Sumer to Modern Iraq.* New York: Atlas & Company, 2008.

"Banned Books Online." The Online Books Page. 28 June 2009. http://digital.library.upenn.edu/books/banned-books.html

"Banned Books: Shakespeare Censored!" Occidental College Library. 1 July 2009. http://departments.oxy.edu/library/geninfo/collections/special/bannedbooks/censoredworks.htm

"The Bible." National Coalition Against Censorship. 29 June 2009. www.thefileroom.org/documents/dyn/DisplayCase.cfm/id/18

Boyer, Paul S. *Purity in Print: Book Censorship in America From the Gilded Age to the Computer Age.* Madison: University of Wisconsin Press, 2002.

"Censorship and Persecution in the Name of Islam." Assyrian International News Agency. 1 Sept. 2007. 29 June 2009. www.aina.org/news/20070108191217.htm

Cherny, Robert W. "The Jungle and the Progressive Era." The Gilder Lehrman Institute of American History. History Now: Books That Changed History. Issue 16. June 2008. 30 June 2009. www.historynow.org/06_2008/historian4.html

Craig, Alec. *Suppressed Books: A History of the Conception of Literary Obscenity.* Cleveland: World Publishing Co., 1963.

"Famed Dramatist, Arthur Miller, Censored and Attacked for Allegedly Criticizing McCarthyism." National Coalition Against Censorship. 29 June 2009. www.thefileroom.org/documents/dyn/DisplayCase.cfm/id/1274

"Fighting the Fires of Hate: America and the Nazi Book Burnings." United States Holocaust Memorial Museum. 1 July 2009. www.ushmm.org/museum/exhibit/online/bookburning/author.php

Foerstel, Herbert N. *Banned in the U.S.A.: A Reference Guide to Book Censorship in Schools and Public Libraries.* Westport, Conn.: Greenwood Press, 2002.

"Frequently Challenged Books of the 21st Century." American Library Association. 30 June 2009. www.ala.org/ala/issuesadvocacy/banned/frequentlychallenged/21stcenturychallenged/index.cfm

Haight, Anne Lyon, and Chandler B. Grannis. *Banned Books, 387 B.C. to 1978 A.D.* New York: R.R. Bowker, 1978.

Howl. Shapes of Time. 1 July 2009. www.shapesoftime.net/pages/viewpage.asp?uniqid=12344

Jones, Derek, ed. *Censorship: A World Encyclopedia.* Chicago: Fitzroy Dearborn Publishers, 2001.

Karolides, Nicholas J., Margaret Bald, and Dawn B. Sova. *120 Banned Books: Censorship Histories and World Literature.* New York: Facts on File, 2005.

Lancto, Craig. "Banned Books: How Schools Restrict the Reading of Young People." The World & I. 2 July 2009. www.worldandi.com/newhome/public/2003/september/mt2pub.asp

"Literary and Historical Notes: Wednesday, 12 April, 2006." The Writer's Almanac With Garrison Keillor. National Public Radio. 1 July 2009. http://writersalmanac.publicradio.org/index.php?date=2006/04/12

Martin, James J. "Other Days, Other Ways: American Book Censorship 1918–1945." Institute for Historical Review. 27 June 2009. www.ihr.org/jhr/v10/v10p133_Martin.html

Mintz, Steven. "Rethinking Huck." The Gilder Lehrman Institute of American History. History Now: Books That Changed History. Issue 16. June 2008. 30 June 2009. www.historynow.org/06_2008/historian3.html

Newth, Mette. "The Long History of Censorship." Beacon for Freedom of Expression. 29 June 2009. www.beaconforfreedom.org/about_project/history.html

Rashidian, Jahanshah. "Book Burning." Iran Press Service. 19 May 2008. 30 June 2009. www.iran-press-service.com/ips/articles-2008/may2008/book-burning.shtml

Riley, Gail Blasser. *Censorship.* New York: Facts on File, 1998.

Robbins, Hollis. "*Uncle Tom's Cabin* and the Matter of Influence." The Gilder Lehrman Institute of American History. History Now: Books That Changed History. Issue 16. June 2008. 30 June 2009. www.historynow.org/06_2008/historian2.html

Scott, A.O. "In Search of the Best." *New York Times Book Review.* 21 May 2006: 17.

Shriver, H.C., and C. Larson. "Books, Bullets, and Blue-Pencils." *Publishers Weekly.* 5 Sept. 1942. Vol. 142: 828–833.

"Top 15 Banned Literary Classics." Listverse. 13 Aug. 2007. 29 June 2009. http://listverse.com/literature/top-15-banned-literary-classics/

Trelease, Jim. "Censors and Children's Literature: Are They Watch Dogs or Mad Dogs?" www.trelease-on-reading.com. 15 Feb. 2009. 29 June 2009. www.trelease-on-reading.com/censor_entry.html

Trelease, Jim. "Talibans and Our Bans." www.trelease-on-reading.com. 14 Nov. 2007. 29 June 2009. www.trelease-on-reading.com/talibanish_bans.html

"Why Books Get Banned, or 'Free People Read Freely.'" BBC. 29 June 2009. www.bbc.co.uk/dna/h2g2/alabaster/A199109

Index

About the Author

Pamela Dell is the author of 60 books for young people, including *Hatshepsut: Egypt's First Female Pharaoh* and several other titles for Compass Point Books. She has also written a historical fiction series and numerous magazine feature articles, and is the author of the monthly fictional series "Doodlebug & Dandelion" in *Spider* magazine. Pamela hangs out mostly in Los Angeles and Chicago and strongly supports everyone's right to read freely.